PROPERTY OF
DAVID S. HORNE O/D HOME

GREAT 20TH CENTURY EXPEDITIONS

HILLARY AND TENZING CLIMB EVEREST

Bob Davidson

A ZOË BOOK

A ZOË BOOK

© 1993 Zoë Books Limited

Devised and produced by
Zoë Books Limited
15 Worthy Lane
Winchester
Hampshire SO23 7AB
England

Apart from any fair dealing for the purposes of research or private study, or criticism or review, as permitted under the Copyright, Designs and Patents Act, 1988, this publication may only be reproduced, stored or transmitted, in any form or by any means, with the prior permission in writing of the publishers, or in the case of reprographic reproduction in accordance with the terms of licences issued by the Copyright Licensing Agency.

Any person who does any unauthorised act in relation to this publication may be liable to criminal prosecution and civil claims for damages.

First published in Great Britain in 1993 by
Zoë Books Limited
15 Worthy Lane
Winchester
Hampshire SO23 7AB

A CIP catalogue record for this book is available from the British Library.

ISBN 1 874488 26 6

Printed in Italy by Grafedit SpA
Design: Jan Sterling, Sterling Associates
Picture research: Faith Perkins
Illustrations and maps: Gecko Limited
Production: Grahame Griffiths

Photographic acknowledgements

The publishers wish to acknowledge, with thanks, the following photographic sources:

The Alpine Club Library: 5b; Chris Bonington: 10, 21, 24, 29b; Dave Clarke: 19b; John Cleare Mountain Camera: 4, 5t, 8 (John English), 12, 13, 14, 20t, 27t, 28, 29t; The Royal Geographical Society: title, 7t, 7b, (David Constantine), 9t (Capt. J. B. Noel), 9b, 11t (Frank Smythe), 11b (M. S. Smythe), 15t,15b, 17t, 17b, 19t, 22, 23t (A Gregory), 23b, 25t; Doug Scott: 25b, 26, 27b

Cover photographs courtesy of Chris Bonington and The Royal Geographical Society (Alfred Gregory)

The publishers have made every effort to trace the copyright holders, but if they have inadvertently overlooked any, they will be pleased to make the necessary arrangement at the first opportunity.

Contents

Climbing high	4
The Himalayas	6
Expeditions in the 1920s	8
Expeditions in the 1930s	10
Everest from the south	12
Planning the 1953 expedition	14
Choosing the equipment	16
The 1953 expedition	18
The ice-fall	20
The final ascent	22
The 'roof of the world'	24
Later expeditions	26
North face solo	28
Glossary	30
Index	32

Climbing high

At around 11.30am on 29 May 1953, two men became the first to reach the highest point in the world – the top of Mount Everest, in Nepal. The two climbers were Edmund Hillary and Tenzing Norgay. They had set out with their team nearly two months earlier. For the final stage of the climb they were on their own. They had been climbing since 6.30am, from their lonely camp 8500 metres (27 900 feet) above sea level. When the tired men saw they had made it to the top, they shook hands then thumped each other on the back in delight. **Mountaineers** had been trying to climb this mountain for 33 years and now Hillary and Tenzing had done it.

'Because it is there'

People who climb high mountains often risk their lives to get to the top. Mountaineers can fall or be blown off the mountainside. Falls of rock and snow, called **avalanches**, can crush and bury them. Yet every year, thousands of people go climbing in the mountains. They enjoy the mountains for many different reasons – the views, the sense of freedom, the excitement. Many people will say they want to get to the top of a mountain simply 'because it is there'.

Mountaineering

It is always extremely cold at the top of high mountains. The temperature is often so low that a climber's fingers and toes can freeze. This causes an injury called **frostbite**, and many mountaineers have lost fingers and toes as a result of it. Most climbers wear special clothes to protect themselves from frostbite. They also use

▼ Mountaineering only began as a sport in 1786, with the climbing of Mont Blanc ('white mountain').

▲ The first successful ascent of the Matterhorn, in the Alps, took place in 1865.

The beginnings of the sport

In 1786, a Frenchman called Michel Paccard from Chamonix, climbed Mont Blanc, at 4807 metres (15 771 feet), the highest mountain in the Alps. Paccard's achievement created a great deal of interest in climbing mountains. Other people began to compete to be the first to climb a particular **peak**.

By the end of the nineteenth century, mountaineers had climbed all the peaks in the Alps. They began to travel to other parts of the world, to find high mountains that had not been climbed before. Mountains in Africa, the Andes (in South America) and the Rockies (in North America) were climbed for the first time. Mountaineers now thought that they had enough skill and knowledge to try to climb some of the highest mountains in the world. Some of the highest peaks are part of the Himalayan **range** of mountains, in Nepal.

equipment such as **ice-axes** and spikes called **crampons** strapped to their boots to help them to grip in icy conditions. Most mountaineers climb in teams and are often roped together to prevent falls.

When people climb in high mountains, they may have difficulty in breathing. At very high levels, or **altitudes**, the air contains less **oxygen**, which people need to breathe properly. Without it, they can quickly become unwell. Usually, this can be prevented by climbing slowly, and gradually getting used to different conditions. This is called being **acclimatised**.

▼ Lucy Walker (in the back row) liked to drink champagne when she was climbing mountains!

The Himalayas

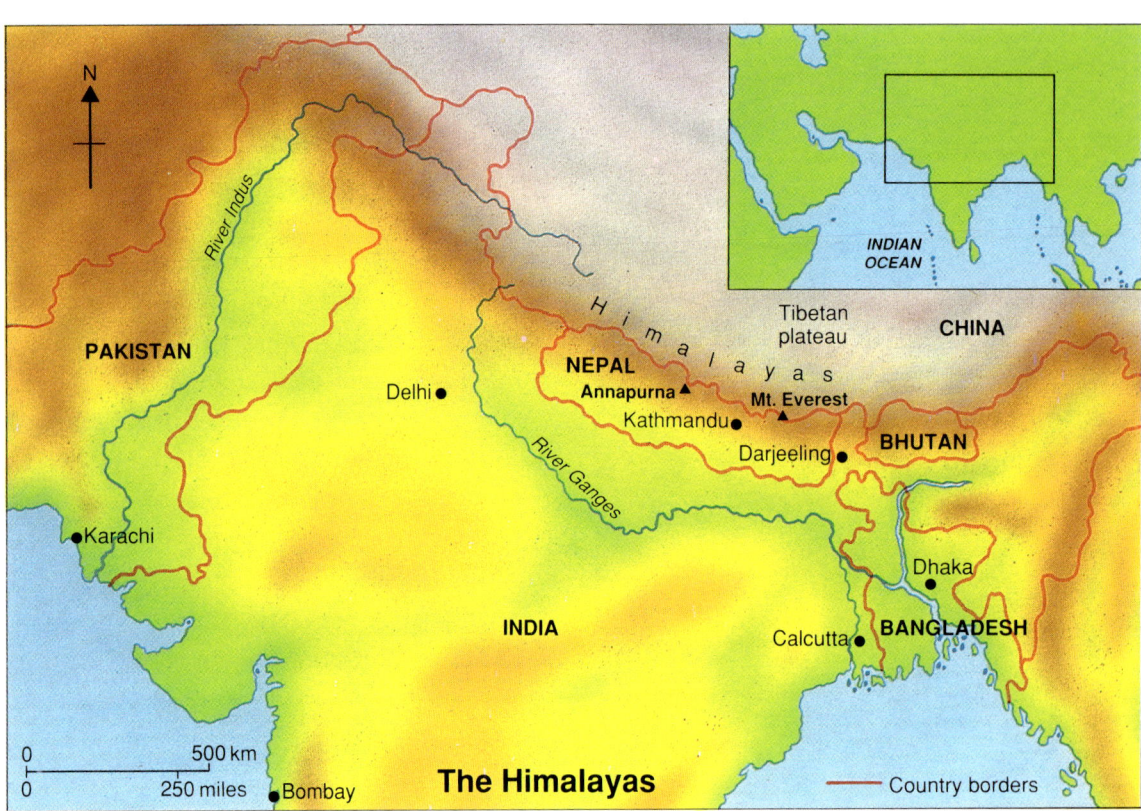

The Himalayas

The groups of mountains which lie between India and China are called the Himalayas. The word 'Himalaya' comes from an ancient Indian language, and means 'snow home'. The Himalayan chain of mountains is about 2400 kilometres (1550 miles) long and 320 kilometres (200 miles) wide. Nearly all these mountain tops, or peaks, are covered in snow all the year round. Many of the peaks are steep and have jagged edges. The high valleys in the mountains often contain rivers of ice. As these rivers move slowly down the slopes, they reach warmer temperatures and begin to melt. These rivers of ice are called **glaciers**.

The northern side of the Himalayas receives little rain and is cold. Much of this land is desert. Most of the rain in the area falls on the southern side of the mountains, and in the summer, the **monsoon** brings weeks of wet weather. The southern side of the mountains is also warmer. On the lower slopes, the flowers, bushes and trees grow very quickly. Some of this land is used for farming or for growing trees.

Very few animals live in the high mountains because it is so cold and there is little to eat. Snow leopards, brown bears and Tibetan yaks are some of the few animals that can survive in the

▲ Mount Everest is named after this British surveyor, Sir George Everest (1790-1866).

mountains. Some insects and spiders can live as high as 6000 metres (20 000 feet).

Nepal

The country of Nepal lies to the northeast of India. Nepal's capital, Kathmandu, is in the centre of the country in one of the few **fertile** areas of land. Most of Nepal is covered by the high mountains of the Himalayas. The people there live in villages scattered along the river valleys.

The highest mountain in the world, Mount Everest, is on the border between Nepal and Tibet.

Mount Everest

Mount Everest is 8848 metres (29 028 feet) high and is surrounded by other very high mountains, with glaciers in the valleys between. The people who live near the mountain have a different name for it. They call the mountain *Chomolungma*, a word used by the Tibetan people that means 'Goddess Mother of the World'.

The twenty year wait

In the 1890s mountaineers turned their attention towards Mount Everest. No mountaineer had been able to get within 100 kilometres (60 miles) of the mountain, to explore the area or to work out how the mountain might be climbed. Everest could only be approached from the north, through Tibet, or from the south, through Nepal. Tibet and Nepal refused to allow any foreigners to travel through their lands, although many requests were made to the rulers of these countries. Finally, in December 1920, Tibet granted permission for one exploration in the Everest region.

▼ An aerial view showing part of the Himalayas

Expeditions in the 1920s

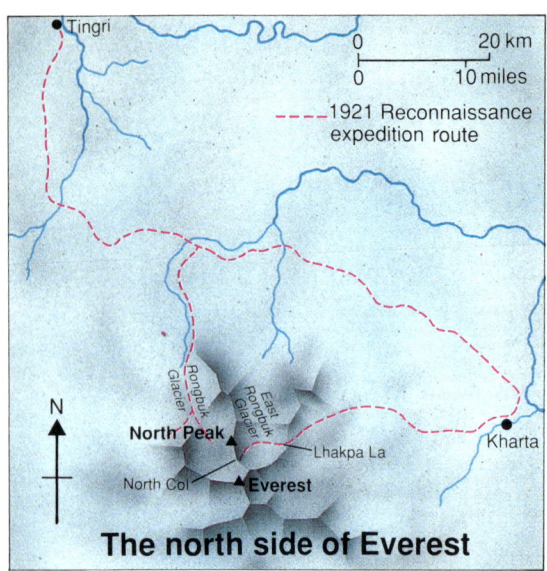

The north side of Everest

In 1921 a British team, including George Mallory, set out on a fact-finding expedition to Mount Everest. Since so little was known about the mountain, the aim of this first trip was to find out as much as possible about conditions in the area. This type of expedition is called a **reconnaissance**.

The team came together in Darjeeling, in India, in May 1921. The distance from Darjeeling to Everest, in a straight line, is about 160 kilometres (100 miles). However the team travelled on foot, and to avoid climbing over many mountains, they could not travel in a straight line! The route they chose meant that they would have to walk 480 kilometres (300 miles) just to reach Everest.

Walking to Everest

For several weeks, they walked through rain-forest, climbed river valleys, crossed mountain passes, and walked across a desert. The expedition had the help of local people to carry most of the supplies and equipment. Some of these were Sherpa people. The Sherpa people come from Northeast Nepal, and are used to mountain conditions. On 19 June, they arrived in the village of Tingri, which they made their base for exploring the northwest side of Everest.

The reconnaissance

The great Rongbuk Glacier drops away northwest of Everest. George Mallory and the climbing team explored the glacier. They thought that a route to the summit might be possible from the North **Col**, but they could not reach the col from the glacier because the climb was too steep. In the end they decided that they could not approach the summit from the northwest.

The team moved their camp to the Kharta Valley. From there they explored the northeast side of Everest. In spite of bad weather, they climbed higher than

▼ Everest, seen from the Rongbuk Glacier

▲ The 1922 expedition having breakfast

they had on the northwest side, but now they were all affected by mountain or **altitude sickness**. They climbed over the Lhakpa La Pass on to the East Rongbuk Glacier, and up to the North Col. It looked possible to reach the summit by climbing the Northeast Ridge from the North Col. However, the winds were strong, and they were all exhausted. They returned to **base camp** and the expedition ended. The team returned to England.

Climbing Everest

Immediately, plans were started for the next expedition. It was to be a serious attempt to reach the summit of Mount Everest. The support team was increased, and this time there would be five climbers, including George Mallory.

On 1 May, 1922, base camp was set up at the foot of the Rongbuk Glacier. The plan was to reach the North Col from the glacier, then to attempt the summit. By 17 May the team had reached the North Col, setting up three camps on the way, and set up Camp 4 at 7000 metres (23 000 feet).

The oxygen, which the team planned to use from now on, had not arrived, and the weather was getting worse. Bravely, they decided to go on without the oxygen. The next day they reached 8100 metres (26 700 feet), but the wind and the cold forced them back to camp. They tried twice more, reaching 8320 metres (27 300 feet), which was a record. Their last attempt ended in disaster when seven Sherpas were killed in an avalanche.

Disaster for Mallory and Irvine

In 1924 a third expedition made another attempt to reach the summit. The mountaineers had increased their knowledge and experience, but they, too, met appalling weather conditions. They were beaten back when they were only 300 metres (1000 feet) from the top. The second attempt ended in tragedy when George Mallory and Andrew Irvine died high on the Northeast Ridge. Again, an expedition returned home without reaching the summit.

▼ George Mallory and Major E F Norton in 1922, climbing the Northeast Ridge.

Expeditions in the 1930s

▲ The north face of Mount Everest. The Northeast Ridge is to the left of the summit.

Tibet remained closed to travellers between 1924 and 1932. Then another expedition was planned for 1933. Since the earlier expeditions, the design of tents, boots and clothes had improved, so the 1933 team was better equipped than any other expedition. The leader of the expedition was Hugh Ruttledge. The number of climbers was increased to fourteen, and they were sure that this time, they would reach the summit of Mount Everest.

The expedition followed the same route as the 1922 and 1924 teams, but they travelled earlier in the year. They reached the top of the East Rongbuk Glacier by early May. For the next three weeks however, they struggled against **blizzards**, hurricanes and snowfalls. Tired and exhausted, two climbers, Wyn Harris and Laurence Wager, reached 8600 metres (28 100 feet) on 30 May. The climb from this point to the summit was too hard for them. There were very steep slopes and

▲ A camp above the North Col, in 1933

they could not be sure that the surface of the snow would support them. If the surface of the snow was unstable, then their lives would be in danger. Yet again, the team had to turn back, less than 300 metres (1000 feet) from the summit.

Shipton's attempts

In 1935 a smaller British team, led by Eric Shipton, approached Mount Everest. The aim of this team was to find out whether the mountain could be climbed during the rainy, or monsoon, period of the year. Earlier expeditions had all failed because of the bad weather in the period which led up to the monsoon. Would the weather be better after the monsoon had started? Would the snow be more stable?

Shipton's team spent some weeks climbing around the north side of the mountain. They decided that an attempt on the summit during the monsoon would be too dangerous. The risk of avalanches was higher, because the warmer weather in June and July was melting the ice and snow.

Although this expedition did not attempt the summit of Mount Everest, they did climb twenty-six other peaks. It took them two months to do this. They also had another look at a possible route up Everest by the West Ridge, but they could not see a way up its lower slopes.

A full expedition in May 1936 tried the route from the North Col to the summit. They failed to make any progress above the North Col because of very bad weather, and they too, returned home unsuccessful.

▼ Eric Shipton on the 1933 expedition

Everest from the south

There were no expeditions in the Everest area during the Second World War, from 1939-1945. In the late 1940s the religious leader of Tibet, the Dalai Lama, would not allow foreigners into the country. After China invaded Tibet in 1950, it seemed unlikely that anyone would be able to approach Everest from the north for some time.

Expeditions in 1949-1950

In 1949, however, a small British expedition was allowed to travel through Nepal, and in 1950, a French climbing team was allowed to travel through Western Nepal. The French climbers made the first ascent of Annapurna, which is 8091 metres (26 545 feet) high. Later in 1950, a team of Americans was allowed to approach the southern side of Everest.

▼ The impressive summit of Annapurna

They made their way up the Khumbu Glacier to the foot of the **ice-fall**. The American expedition did not find out any more about the possibility of reaching the summit of Everest from the south. They did, however, succeed in getting permission to cross Nepal. This was an important step in gaining access to Mount Everest again.

The 1951 reconnaissance

In June 1951, a team of eight climbers received permission to approach the south side of Everest. This team included Eric Shipton and a New Zealander, Edmund Hillary.

The team wanted to find out whether they could climb the ice-fall into the Western **Cwm**. If they could, they would then try to reach the eastern end of the cwm. From there, they would be able to see whether there was a route up the South Col, and along the Southeast Ridge to Everest's summit.

The expedition travelled to Everest in September 1951. They did manage to climb, or scale, the ice-fall, but they were unable to go any further. The glacier in the Western Cwm was split by very large cracks, or **crevasses**, and the team could not cross them. Instead, they climbed the slopes on the western side of the Khumbu Glacier, and looked up the Western Cwm above the ice-fall. From there, they saw that it would be possible to reach the bottom of the slopes below the South Col.

The southwest approach to Everest

When the expedition returned to England, they were sure that the ice-fall could be climbed, and that there was a route through the Western Cwm. They were still unsure as to whether there was a route to the summit by the South Col and Southeast Ridge.

1952 – the Swiss take up the challenge

In May 1952, a Swiss climbing team took the route over the ice-fall and along the Western Cwm to the foot of the Geneva Spur. They climbed to the South Col and, in spite of bad weather, they climbed the Southeast Ridge to within 240 metres (800 feet) of the summit. Then they had to return, driven back by bad weather and lack of supplies.

▶ A climber at the foot of the ice-fall

Planning the 1953 expedition

▲ The summit of Everest is to the left of the South Col, which is in the centre of the skyline.

All the British expeditions to Everest were organised by a group of people who were based in London. The Everest group, or committee, was made up of members of the Alpine Club and the Royal Geographic Society. They raised the money for the expeditions from wealthy people, or businesses, who were interested in helping a British team to be first to the top of Everest. *The Times* newspaper was among the expedition's supporters, and the Duke of Edinburgh agreed to be the patron of the expedition.

Hunt's plan of attack

In September 1952, the Everest Committee chose Colonel John Hunt to lead the 1953 expedition. John Hunt was 42 years old, and a British soldier. He had a great deal of experience of climbing in snow and icy conditions in the Himalayas. It was Hunt's job to prepare a plan, or strategy, for the 1953 expedition. It was very important to have the right plan, because the success or failure of the attempt depended on it. If the plan did not work, then not only would the team fail to reach the summit of Everest, but their lives would be in danger.

Hunt felt sure that the route the Swiss team had taken in 1952 was the right one. He also knew that the key to success lay in having climbers who were properly acclimatised. They also had to have enough supplies, and these had to be as far up the mountain as possible. He aimed to be at the South Col before the monsoon arrived in June. The good weather before

▲ The members of the 1953 expedition

the monsoon usually lasted for about two weeks from the end of May to the middle of June, and in that time, Hunt hoped to attempt the summit from the South Col.

This was Hunt's plan – now he had to find the climbers!

Choosing the team

Hunt needed climbers who had experience of climbing in the Alps, or better still, in the Himalayas. They had to be used to the icy conditions that they would meet on Everest. They had to be very strong and fit. In addition, they had to be climbers who would make a good team and would work well together. Above all, they had to be determined to get to the top!

Hunt chose seven climbers from Britain and two from New Zealand. The British climbers were Charles Evans, Tom Bourdillon, Alfred Gregory, Charles Wylie, Michael Westmacott, George Band and Wilfred Noyce. Edmund Hillary and George Lowe came from New Zealand. To complete the team, Hunt selected three other climbers. Michael Ward would be the team doctor. A scientist, Griffith Pugh, would study the effects of altitude on the human body. Tom Stobart would take a film of the expedition. The money raised from showing the film would help to pay for the expedition.

A team of Sherpas would also be used to provide support for the climbers at high altitude. Hunt knew the man he wanted to lead the Sherpas. He was an expert mountaineer called Tenzing Norgay.

▼ Edmund Hillary learned his mountaineering skills climbing in New Zealand.

Choosing the equipment

Hunt was determined that the expedition would not fail because of poor equipment. He chose the best that he could find. Everything had to be light, and had to work even in strong winds and the bitter cold of the mountains.

Hunt's team tested many of the latest designs in clothes, tents, boots and sleeping-bags. They decided to live on army food, which was carefully planned to give soldiers strength and keep them alive! To cook they would use 22 paraffin stoves and six gas stoves.

Mountaineering equipment

Thousands of metres of the best climbing rope, as well as ice-hammers and axes, **pitons** and **snap links**, were obtained. The team needed ladders to help them cross any crevasses. One ladder was rope, the other was made of metal and could be carried in sections. They also borrowed a mortar gun from the British Army. They could fire the gun to clear any loose snow which might be ahead of them. In this way they hoped to be safe from sudden avalanches.

The oxygen equipment was most important. It had to be light, and needed to last a long time. Again, the team took the best equipment they could find.

▼ The oxygen equipment was very important because it helped the climbers to reach high altitudes without becoming ill. The expedition took three different types of oxygen sets with them. The open-circuit and closed-circuit sets were for use when climbing. The third set, a sleeping set, was for use at night to help the climbers to breathe properly while sleeping. The open-circuit set is shown here.

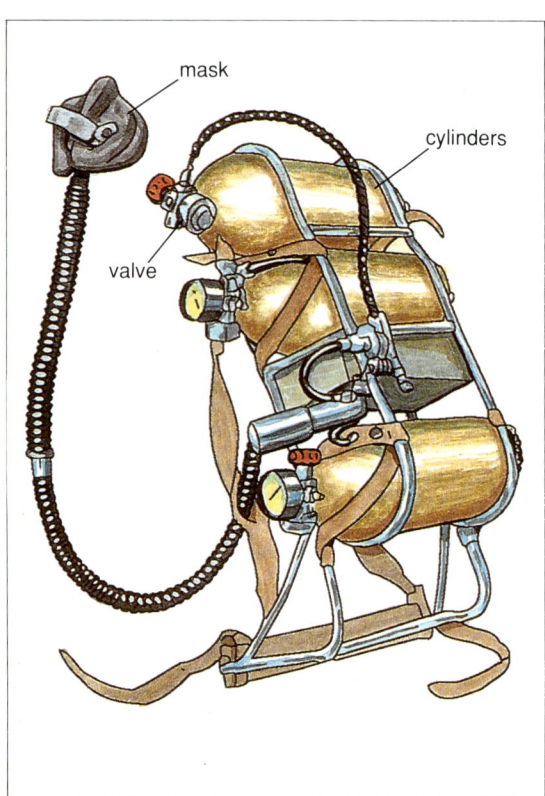

Keeping in touch

The team took eight walkie-talkie handsets with them, so that they could talk to each other on the mountain. These sets operated up to three kilometres (two miles) apart. They also took a short-wave radio, so that they could receive weather forecasts from a radio station in India. The All-India Radio agreed to send them special weather information, which would be very important for day-to-day planning on the mountain.

▲ John Hunt testing the portable radio

Final preparations

Some of the equipment, such as the oxygen, was tested during the winter of 1952 in North Wales and in the Alps. Before leaving for India, Hunt visited Buckingham Palace and met the Duke of Edinburgh, the patron of the expedition. The Duke wished the team well. On 12 February 1953, the team with all their equipment, sailed for Bombay in India.

▼ The supplies required for the Everest expedition just fit into a small field!

The 1953 expedition

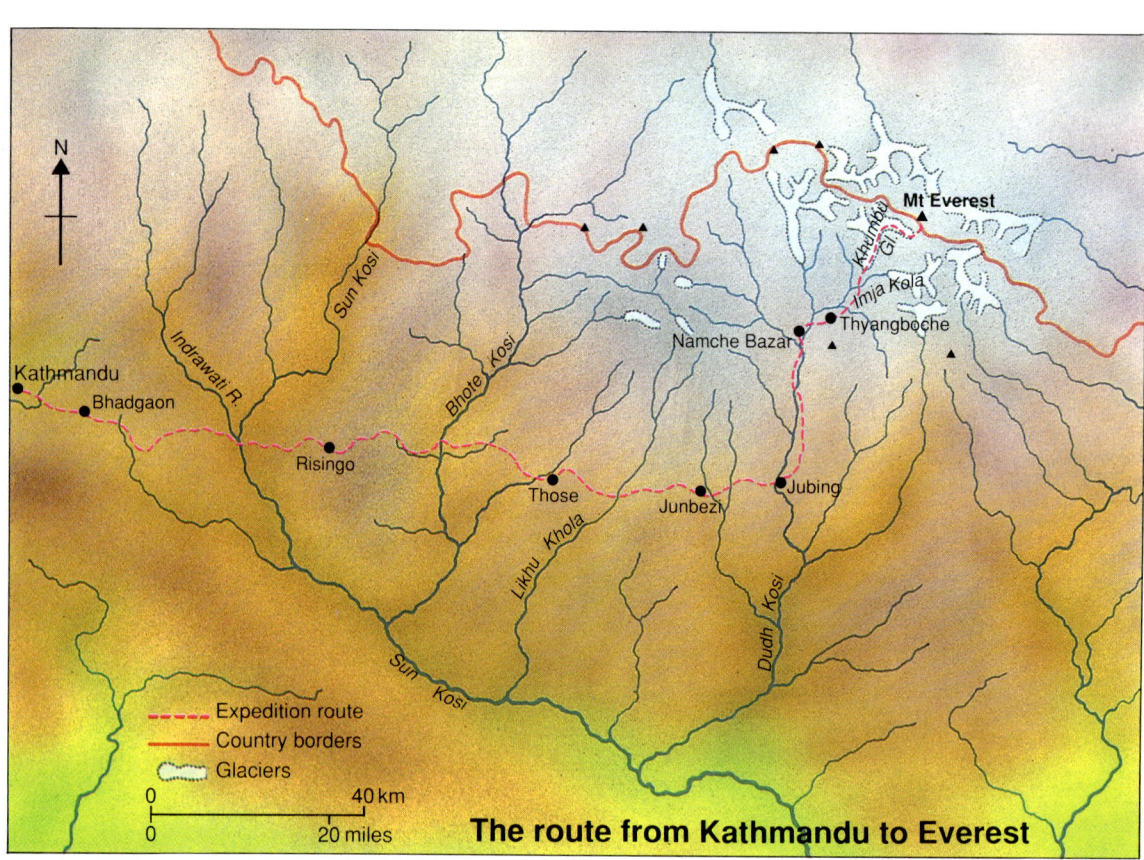

The route from Kathmandu to Everest

The expedition travelled across India from Bombay to Kathmandu in Nepal. In Kathmandu they hired 350 people to carry their equipment into the mountains. It was here that Tenzing Norgay also joined the expedition. The team left Kathmandu in early March, heading for Mount Everest.

To Thyangboche

In good spring weather, the expedition walked eastwards. They climbed hills and walked through woods and valleys. Sometimes they crossed foaming rivers. The countryside of Nepal was beautiful, but the walkers were thinking ahead. They knew that snow, ice and bitter winds were waiting for them in the high mountains. On the journey, they began to acclimatise to the height. They also practised wearing oxygen masks for a few hours each day.

After seventeen days of walking, the team reached the **monastery** at Thyangboche. It is more than 3660 metres (12 000 feet) above sea level, and is thought to be the highest monastery in the world. The monastery is near the Imja Kola River, which is one of the main rivers flowing south from the mountains near Everest.

▲ Members of the 1953 expedition set up camp below the monastery at Thyangboche.

In training

Thyangboche was the team's base for three weeks of training. They needed to acclimatise properly before they began to climb Everest. So they climbed a number of mountains, up to heights of 5800 metres (19 000 feet). They also practised climbing together as a team, and climbing with their oxygen.

The Khumbu Glacier

On 8 April, the first team of four climbers left Thyangboche. This advance party followed the Imja Kola River for about 6.5 kilometres (four miles), then they turned north. They were now in the bleak valley of the Lobujya Khola River, which flows from the Khumbu Glacier.

Their progress was slow, because new snow had fallen before they reached the glacier. They had to climb through a jumble of boulders, called **glacial moraine**, and they walked through a 'forest' of tall ice spikes, or **seracs**. It took them four days to reach the foot of the ice-fall, at 5500 metres (18 000 feet). There they set up camp. Several days later, the rest of the expedition joined the advance party.

▼ The Khumbu Glacier

The ice-fall

▲ A breathtaking view of the ice-fall

The ice-fall at the head of the Khumbu Glacier is like a giant, frozen waterfall. The ice-fall drops steeply for about 600 metres (2000 feet) from the end of the Western Cwm to the glacier below. There are crevasses in the ice, which change shape as the ice drops slowly. Huge icicles hang down dangerously, and enormous seracs jut out from the ice-fall. These seracs often topple over and crash down the ice-fall.

Climbing the ice

Hunt could not plan a route up the slope, because the shape of the ice-fall changes so often. Hillary led a party up the slope, and decided that the easiest and safest route lay up the middle of the ice-fall. There, the climbers would be out of the path of avalanches which might fall from either side.

The team made slow progress up the ice-fall. They had to use their axes to chip out hand-holds and steps, and sometimes they had to cut a staircase in the ice. This would be used by those who were following with all the supplies. The team also had to build bridges across some of the wider crevasses. They used some of the sections of their metal ladder for the bridges.

After three days they reached the halfway point up the ice-fall, and made a camp on a ledge of ice. When they moved

▼ The route of the expedition through the Western Cwm, and up to the summit

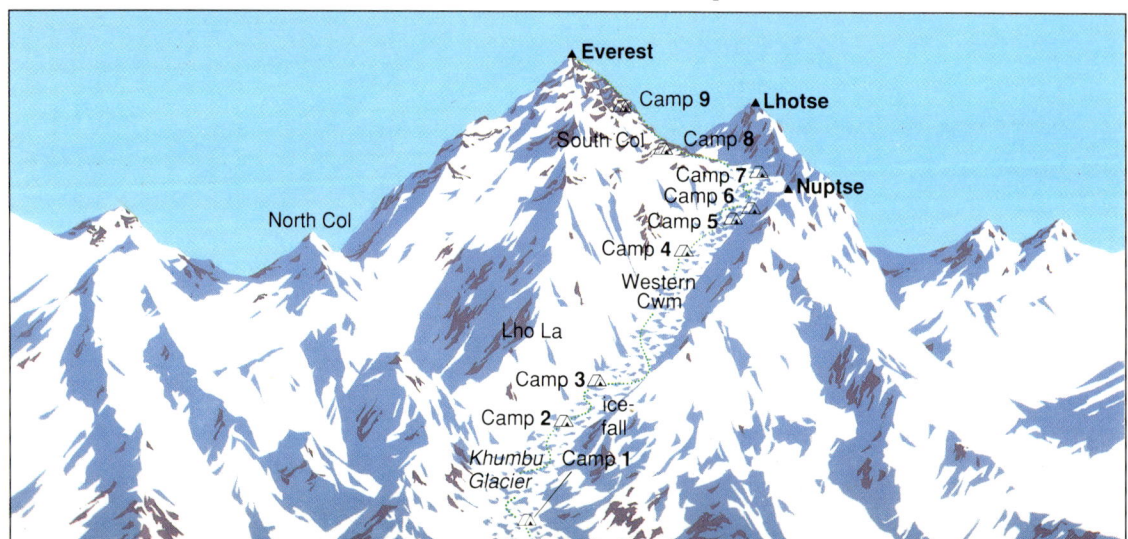

▲ Mountaineers in the Western Cwm heading towards the foot of the west face of Lhotse.

on, there were snowfalls, which slowed them even more. It took them another seven days to reach the top of the ice-fall. There the team set up Camp 3, at 6160 metres (20 200 feet).

The Western Cwm

The Western Cwm is a wild and eerie place. It is about three kilometres (two miles) long and up to two kilometres (one mile) wide. It drops towards the ice-fall, and is surrounded on three sides by mountains – Everest, Lhotse and Nuptse. Nothing grows in the cwm, because it is so high, and snow falls regularly. The cwm is split by crevasses, and is bombarded by avalanches from the mountains above.

The head of the cwm

The way into the cwm from Camp 3 was split by wide crevasses. Once again, the team had to use their ladders to cross them. When they were in the cwm, they made good progress, leaving marker flags to show the route they had taken, in case there were heavy snowfalls. On 1 May they set up Camp 4 at 6460 metres (21 200 feet), and two days later, they reached the west face of Lhotse, where they set up Camp 5.

Camp 4 was to be the base camp for the final climb to the top of Everest. All the supplies for the next three weeks were brought up to Camp 4 by the Sherpas. They carried 45 loads, each weighing about 18 kilograms (40 pounds), over the ice-fall and along the Cwm.

Lhotse face

The team chose a route up the west face of Lhotse to reach the South Col, and it took ten days to make this ascent. Snowfalls and high winds held the team back. They pitched two camps, 6 and 7, on ledges on the sides of the mountain, to provide support for the climbers. By 21 May, they had reached the South Col and set up Camp 8.

The final ascent

Hunt planned that two teams would make separate attempts to reach the summit of Everest from the South Col. The first team was to climb to the 'South Summit', which was 100 metres (300 feet) below the real summit. The last stage was hidden from the South Col by the South Summit, so no one knew what the last climb would be like. If the first team reached the South Summit and was able to go on, the climbers would try to reach the top. If they failed, the other team would make the second attempt. In all, the summit of Everest is 1000 metres (3000 feet) above the South Col.

The climbers in the first team were Tom Bourdillon and Charles Evans. In the second team, the climbers were Edmund Hillary and Tenzing Norgay.

The first attempt

On 26 May, Bourdillon and Evans left the South Col. They were followed by Hunt and Sherpa Da Namgyal, who carried a tent, food and fuel up the Southeast Ridge. At 8340 metres (27 350 feet), Hunt and Da Namgyal became exhausted, and returned to the South Col.

Bourdillon and Evans reached the top of the South Summit, in spite of some difficulties with snowfalls. From there they could see the final ridge, and they decided that it could be climbed. They were now at 8750 metres (28 700 feet) – higher than anyone had climbed before.

▼ Bourdillon and Evans after their climb

▲ Hillary and Tenzing climbing up towards the Southeast Ridge from Camp 8.

However, they had neither strength nor oxygen to carry on to the top, so they returned to Camp 8. They did leave two bottles of oxygen behind, to help the following team.

The second attempt

The wind was so strong the next day, 27 May, that no attempt could be made. On 28 May, Hillary and Tenzing, with Lowe, Gregory and Sherpa Ang Nima, climbed the Southeast Ridge. They collected the equipment which Hunt and Da Namgyal had left, and climbed slowly to 8500 metres (27 900 feet). Then Lowe, Gregory and Ang Nima returned to the South Col.

Hillary and Tenzing cleared snow from the rocks and set up Camp 9. They boiled snow to make hot drinks, and as the sun set, they ate sardines, biscuits, tinned apricots, dates, jam and honey. The apricots had to be thawed out, as they had frozen solid in the tin. The two climbers then settled to sleep in the highest camp in the world.

At 4.00 am they rose to discover that Hillary's boots had also frozen solid. The boots had to be thawed out over the stove, along with breakfast! By 6.30 am the climbers were ready to set out. Carrying 14 kilograms (30 pounds) of oxygen equipment, they headed for the South Summit. Using their ice-axes to cut steps, they reached the South Summit by 9 am. The weather was good and they had plenty of oxygen left. It was time to try to reach the summit of Everest.

▼ The summit ridge from the South Summit

The 'roof of the world'

▲ Mountaineers approaching the 'Hillary Step' on the summit ridge.

Hillary and Tenzing climbed for about an hour beyond the South Summit. Then they came to what looked like a sheer cliff face. The cliff was about 12 metres (40 feet) high, and the rock was smooth. They did not think that they could climb up the cliff, but neither could they go round it. After some minutes of staring closely at the cliff, Hillary saw a small crack, running up the side of the cliff face. He wedged himself into the crack, and began to kick steps in the ice at the side of the cliff with his crampons. Slowly and painfully Hillary levered himself up to the top of the cliff. Tenzing followed him, a few minutes later. This cliff is now known as the 'Hillary **Step**'.

At the top!

Hillary and Tenzing continued along the ridge, cutting steps with their ice-axes on the narrow strip of snow. The ridge seemed never-ending. After two hours, they were still cutting steps, and they were both tiring. After every hump in the ridge, there was another, still higher. Suddenly, Hillary noticed that the next hump was lower than the one he was on. They were at the top!

On the summit of Everest

Hillary said that his first feelings were of relief – no more climbing! He looked at Tenzing, and knew that underneath his balaclava helmet, goggles and oxygen

▲ Tenzing Norgay on the summit

mask, Tenzing was grinning! The two shook hands and thumped each other on the back with delight. They switched off their oxygen, took photographs and enjoyed the wonderful view. Tenzing made a hole in the snow. As a Buddhist, he marked the moment by burying some small items of food in the snow. Hillary put a small cross, or crucifix, which had been given to him by Hunt, into the hole.

They had reached the top at 11.30 am, and after fifteen minutes, they started back down the mountain. They picked up the oxygen which was left by Bourdillon and Evans, and reached Camp 9 by mid-afternoon. There they melted snow and made a sugary lemon drink – by now they felt weak and exhausted. They moved on down towards the South Col, cutting steps as they went. At last, excited but weary, they reached Camp 8 – by this time they were almost too tired to speak.

The following day, the expedition began to leave the mountain tops. By 2 June, all the climbers were back at base camp. From there, they returned to Kathmandu and then to London, where they were given a heroes' welcome in early July. The news of the expedition's success reached London on 2 June 1953 – the day of the coronation of Queen Elizabeth II.

▼ A view from the highest point on Earth

Later expeditions

▲ Looking back from the summit towards the South Summit, with Lhotse on the left

Everest has been climbed many times since the 1953 expedition. New routes to the top have been tried, often successfully. However, many climbers have died in the last 40 years while trying to reach the summit.

Breaking records

The first successful climb from the North Col was made by a Chinese team in 1960. There were 214 mountaineers involved in this expedition.

Then in 1963 an American team climbed to the summit for the first time from the West Ridge. They came down the mountain by the South Col route, which meant that they were the first team to cross, or **traverse**, Everest. Another American, Dick Bass, reached the top of Everest at the age of 55 years. He was the oldest climber to have scaled the mountain. Bass was also the first mountaineer to have climbed the highest peaks of every continent in the world.

▲ Wanda Rutkiewicz

In May 1975, Junko Tabei from Japan became the first woman to climb Everest. The first European woman to climb Everest was Wanda Rutkiewicz, a Polish mountaineer. Rutkiewicz was also part of an all-women's expedition in 1985 which successfully ascended Nanga Parbat. Nanga Parbat is a mountain in the northeast of Pakistan, and is 8125 metres (26600 feet) high.

The southwest face of Everest

In 1975, the British climber Chris Bonington led a team of climbers up Everest from the Western Cwm. This climb had been tried five times before, but without success. None of the attempts had been able to cross a large band of rock which stretches across the southwest face of Everest. Bonington planned to cross this band at its narrowest point, and to make sure that his team had enough support on the mountain.

One of Bonington's team, Nick Estcourt, finally found a way through the band. It took a great deal of courage and determination to do this. Five climbers reached the top of Everest in that expedition. Sadly, one of the climbers, Mick Burke, was trapped in a blizzard on the top and died on the descent.

▼ A camp on the southwest face, in 1975

North face solo

In 1980, an Austrian climber, Reinhold Messner, climbed the north face of Everest alone! He approached the summit from the East Rongbuk Glacier, then climbed to the North Col and reached the summit by crossing the north face of the mountain. Messner said that the last few metres of the climb were 'agony; I have never in my life been so tired as on the summit of Mount Everest that day'. Messner had to crawl these last few metres on his hands and knees.

▼ Reinhold Messner

Reinhold Messner was also one of the first climbers to reach the top of Everest without using oxygen. In 1986, he became the first person to have climbed all fourteen peaks in the world which are more than 8000 metres (26 250 feet) high.

Lhotse

In 1956, a Swiss climbing team was the first to climb Everest after Hillary and Tenzing. They went on to make the first ascent of Lhotse, from the north.

Several attempts were made to climb this mountain from the south in the 1970s and 1980s, but all of them failed. Even Reinhold Messner twice failed to climb Lhotse. He called the south face of the mountain, 'a climb for the twenty-first century'. In 1990, a young climber from Slovenia, Tomo Česen, attempted the south face of Lhotse.

Česen spent a long time preparing for his attempt. He read about other climbs on Lhotse, and he studied the south face from the mountains nearby. Finally Česen decided that he would climb alone, since he thought that it would be quicker and easier to do it that way. He also knew that to climb in daylight would be dangerous, because the sun melted the ice and caused rock falls. So Česen climbed alone, and mostly at night. After three days on the mountain, he reached the top in wind and snow. He had climbed one of the most difficult peaks in the world, and he had done it alone. His success was one of the

▲ The towering south face of Lhotse

◄ Tomo Česen

greatest achievements in the history of mountaineering.

The future of mountaineering

The skill of mountaineers continues to improve. The bravery and the successes of climbers such as Mallory, Shipton, Tenzing and Hillary have inspired many mountaineers, such as Messner and Česen. Climbers will attempt, and achieve, what was thought to be impossible. Perhaps there is now no such thing as 'an impossible climb'.

Glossary

acclimatise:	to become used to new conditions
altitude:	height, usually above sea level
altitude sickness:	an illness caused by the lack of oxygen in the air at high altitudes. It can be avoided by acclimatisation and by drinking plenty of liquids.
avalanche:	sudden movement of large amounts of snow, ice and stones down a mountain
base camp:	the main camp for an expedition. Food and equipment are stored here for use later on in the expedition.
blizzard:	a storm of wind and snow
col:	a dip in a mountain chain
crampon:	a metal frame with spikes, fitting the sole of the boot, for use on hard snow or ice
crevasse:	a crack in a glacier, often very deep
cwm:	an enclosed valley on the side of a hill
fertile:	describes rich soil where seeds and plants can grow well
frostbite:	permanent damage to skin caused by low or freezing temperatures
glacial moraine:	a collection of rocks, stones and soil that is carried by a glacier for some distance and then left at the edges of it
glacier:	a 'river' of ice, often several kilometres long, moving very slowly down a mountain
ice-axe:	an axe used by mountain climbers to cut steps in ice
ice-fall:	a steep fall in a glacier, where many cracks and ice pinnacles develop
monastery:	a place where monks live together
monsoon:	a strong wind from the Indian Ocean, that brings very heavy rain to parts of Southeast Asia at certain times of the year
mountaineer:	a person who climbs mountains as a sport

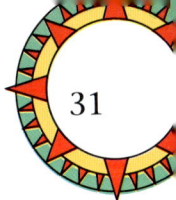

oxygen:	a gas that humans and animals need to breathe, in order to stay alive
peak:	the top of a pointed mountain
piton:	a metal peg hammered into a crack in a rock to support a rope
range:	a group or row of, for example, mountains
reconnaissance:	the first trip or survey to gather information about an area
serac:	a pinnacle or tower of ice, that is often unsafe
snap link:	a metal clip used to secure a rope safely
step:	a short, steep part of a mountain
traverse:	to move horizontally or diagonally across a mountain slope. It can also mean the ascent and descent of a mountain by different routes.

Further Reading

The Ascent of Everest, by John Hunt (Hodder and Stoughton, 1953)

The Story of Everest, by W.H. Murray (J.M. Dent & Sons, 1953)

Everest The Hard Way, by Chris Bonington (Hodder and Stoughton, 1976)

The Everest Years, by Chris Bonington (Hodder and Stoughton, 1986)

High Adventure, by Edmund Hillary (Hodder and Stoughton, 1955)

The Crystal Horizon: Everest, the first solo ascent, by Reinhold Messner (Crowood Press, 1989)

The Climbers, by Chris Bonington (BBC Books and Hodder and Stoughton, 1992)

Index

acclimatisation 5, 14, 18, 19
altitude 5, 15
altitude sickness 9
Ang Nima 23
Annapurna 12
avalanche 4, 9, 11, 16, 20, 21
Band, George 15
Bass, Dick 26
blizzard 10, 27
Bonington, Chris 27
Bourdillon, Tom 15, 22, 23, 25
Česen, Tomo 28, 29
clothing 4, 16
cooking equipment 16, 23
crampon 5, 24
crevasse 12, 16, 20, 21
Da Namgyal 22, 23
Dalai Lama 12
Duke of Edinburgh 14, 17
East Rongbuk Glacier 9, 10, 28
Evans, Charles 15, 22, 23, 25
Everest Committee 14
food 16, 23, 25
frostbite 4
Geneva Spur 13
Gregory, Alfred 15, 23
Hillary, Edmund 4, 12, 15, 20, 22-25, 28, 29
'Hillary Step' 24
Hunt, John 14-17, 20, 22, 23, 25
ice-axe 5, 16, 20, 23, 24
ice-fall 12, 13, 19-21
Imja Kola River 18, 19
Irvine, Andrew 9
Kathmandu 7, 18, 25
Khumbu Glacier 12, 19, 20
ladders 16, 20, 21

Lhotse 21, 26, 28, 29
Lowe, George 15, 23
Mallory, George 8, 9, 29
Matterhorn 5
Messner, Reinhold 28, 29
monsoon 6, 11, 14, 15
Mont Blanc 4, 5
Nanga Parbat 27
Nepal 4, 5, 7, 8, 12, 18
North Col 8, 9, 11, 26, 28
Northeast Ridge 9, 10
Noyce, Wilfred 15
Nuptse 21
oxygen 5, 9, 16-19, 23-25, 28
Paccard, Michel 5
piton 16
reconnaissance 8
Rongbuk Glacier 8, 9
Rutkiewicz, Wanda 27
serac 19, 20
Sherpas 8, 9, 15, 21, 22, 23
Shipton, Eric 11, 12, 29
snap link 16
South Col 12-15, 21-23, 25, 26
South Summit 22-24, 26
Southeast Ridge 12, 13, 22, 23
southwest face 27
Tabei, Junko 27
Tenzing Norgay 4, 15, 18, 22-25, 28, 29
Thyangboche 18, 19
Tibet 7, 10, 12
Walker, Lucy 5
West Ridge 11, 26
Western Cwm 12, 13, 20, 21, 27
Westmacott, Michael 15
Wylie, Charles 15